Wishes, Advice, and Happy Thoughts for Your

MARRIAGE

For _____ from us

Additional Thoughts

_____

_____

_____

_____

_____

_____

_____

_____

When I found out you two were getting hitched, I

_____!

With love, _____

Additional Thoughts

_____

_____

_____

_____

_____

_____

_____

_____

I've known you

———————————————————————,

and I can honestly say, I've never seen you more

———————————————————————.

With love, ————————————

Additional Thoughts

It's normal to feel a little

_____

on your wedding day! Just remember

_____.

With love, _____

Additional Thoughts

_____

_____

_____

_____

_____

_____

_____

_____

I'd love to give you two a lifetime supply of

_____

and

_____.

With love, _____

Additional Thoughts

I can't wait to see you guys

_____ .

With love, _____

Additional Thoughts

_____

_____

_____

_____

_____

_____

_____

_____

The best marriage advice I ever got was

_____ .

With love, _____

Additional Thoughts

_____

_____

_____

_____

_____

_____

_____

_____

I know your wedding is going to be

_____,

just like you.

With love, _____

Additional Thoughts

_____

_____

_____

_____

_____

_____

_____

_____

You were already a great couple, but now you're

_____!

With love, _____

Additional Thoughts

The story of how you two

_____

is the best.

With love, _____

Additional Thoughts

_____

_____

_____

_____

_____

_____

_____

_____

I love to see the joy you two take in

_____ .

With love, _____

Additional Thoughts

Never underestimate the power of

_____ .

With love, _____

Additional Thoughts

_____

_____

_____

_____

_____

_____

_____

_____

Try to avoid having serious discussions when

_____ .

With love, _____

Additional Thoughts

I hope your wedding night is

_____ .

With love, _____

Additional Thoughts

_____

_____

_____

_____

_____

_____

_____

_____

No matter how busy your lives get, try to

_____

every day.

With love, _____

Additional Thoughts

_____

_____

_____

_____

_____

_____

_____

_____

_____

is lucky to be living with such a talented

_____!

With love, _____

Additional Thoughts

_____

_____

_____

_____

_____

_____

_____

_____

_____

is lucky to be living with such a gifted

_____!

With love, _____

Additional Thoughts

If one of you makes dinner, the other should

_____.

With love, _____

Additional Thoughts

I hope your honeymoon includes lots of

_____

and no

_____ .

With love, _____

Additional Thoughts

It's always okay to admit

———————————————————.

With love, ——————————

Additional Thoughts

_____

_____

_____

_____

_____

_____

_____

_____

My favorite memory of you two is

_____ .

With love, _____

Additional Thoughts

_____

_____

_____

_____

_____

_____

_____

_____

Always trust

_____.

With love, _____

Additional Thoughts

I really admire how you two

_____ .

With love, _____

Additional Thoughts

_____

_____

_____

_____

_____

_____

_____

_____

Try to

_____

without phones or other distractions.

With love, _____

Additional Thoughts

Despite your love for each
other, it's best to use separate

_____ .

With love, _____

Additional Thoughts

_____

_____

_____

_____

_____

_____

_____

_____

I hope you two get to

_____

at least once a year.

With love, _____

Additional Thoughts

_____

_____

_____

_____

_____

_____

_____

_____

I hope you two get to

_____

at least once a month.

With love, _____

Additional Thoughts

I hope you two get to

_____

at least once a week.

With love, _____

Additional Thoughts

Never try to assemble furniture when

_____ .

With love, _____

Additional Thoughts

_____

_____

_____

_____

_____

_____

_____

_____

You are such a

_____,

I know your life together will be full of

_____.

With love, _____

Additional Thoughts

Don't listen to anyone who tells you

_____ .

With love, _____

Additional Thoughts

_____

_____

_____

_____

_____

_____

_____

_____

It's perfectly fine to have wildly different taste in

_____!

With love, _____

Additional Thoughts

_____

_____

_____

_____

_____

_____

_____

_____

As a couple, you make the world

_____ .

With love, _____

Additional Thoughts

_____

_____

_____

_____

_____

_____

_____

_____

Try not to go longer than

_____

without

_____ .

With love, _____

Additional Thoughts

If you get things you don't want or need for
wedding gifts, you should feel no shame in

_____ .

With love, _____

Additional Thoughts

I can't wait to see what happens when

_____ .

With love, _____

Additional Thoughts

Never go to bed

_____ .

With love, _____

Additional Thoughts

You two are going to have so much fun

_____.

With love, _____

Additional Thoughts

_____

_____

_____

_____

_____

_____

_____

_____

I wish nothing but

_____

for your family.

With love, _____

Congratulations,

_____!

Guest	Gift	Address/Notes

Guest	Gift	Address/Notes

Guest	Gift	Address/Notes

Guest	Gift	Address/Notes

Guest	Gift	Address/Notes

Guest	Gift	Address/Notes

Guest	Gift	Address/Notes

Fill in the *Love.*®

Created, published, and distributed by Knock Knock
6080 Center Drive
Los Angeles, CA 90045
knockknockstuff.com
Knock Knock is a registered trademark of Knock Knock LLC
Fill in the Love is a registered trademark of Knock Knock LLC

ISBN: 978-168349050-0
UPC: 825703-50261-9

10 9 8 7 6 5 4 3